Ian is six.

"I have a seed for you, Ian," said Grandma.

"I will put in the seed," said Ian.

"Then I will have a plant."

"You will," said Grandma.
"Plants need time, Ian."

"The plant is not up!" said Ian.

"Plants need time, Ian," said Father.

"The plant is not up!" said Ian.

"Plants need time, Ian," said Mother.

Then the plant came up.
It came up and up and UP!

"We will fix my plant," said Ian.
"We will put it out."

And out it went.